ON FLAT-RATE TAX PROPOSALS

By
Michael A. Walker
Director, The Fraser Institute

FOCUS NO. 4

1983

ISBN 0-88975-058-0

CONTENTS

ON FLAT-RATE TAX PROPOSALS

1. INTEREST IN THE FLAT-RATE TAX

Almost every Canadian is aware of the economic debacle which was the November 1981 budget of then Finance Minister MacEachen. Every uncomplimentary adjective imaginable has adorned it. While much of the criticism of that budget has been intemperate, there can be no question but that its overall thrust has been quite accurate. In part, as a reflection of these telling critiques the budget has been withdrawn almost in its entirety, partly by MacEachen and partly by his successor, Finance Minister Lalonde.

There was within Mr. MacEachen's budget a principle of reform which has received very little acknowledgement in Canada but which is receiving a considerable amount of attention in the United States. This neglected aspect of the MacEachen budget is a fundamentally sound and desirable target for policy -- that is, the objective of achieving a flat tax system or at least a flatter tax system, along with a considerable reduction in the complexity of deductions and exemptions. (At the time of writing, there were 10 bills proposing various flat tax configurations before the U.S. Congress. See Appendix.)

The purpose of this paper is to examine the quantitative issues involved in a flat-rate tax system and to determine what would be the effects of the adoption of such a system in Canada. Evidently, many of the problems involved in the adoption of such a system are political and involve the activities of pressure groups, and special interests. It is not the intention of this paper to consider the political ramifications of a flat-rate tax. Moreover, this paper should be regarded as a preliminary assessment rather than the final word.

Flatten the tax or plug the loopholes

Both the MacEachen budget and the tax proposals currently being advanced in the United States have the characteristic that they involve two distinct elements of tax reform. The first element is the lowering of the average tax rate faced by taxpayers and the elimination of a progression from lower to higher rates of tax as income increases. The second element involves the definition of taxable income. That is to say, what will taxpayers be able to deduct from their gross income to determine their taxable income? Now, it is clearly the case that these two elements of the proposed reforms are not necessarily interdependent. There could be an elimination of the progressivity of the tax system and the adoption of a flat-rate of tax regardless of income with no change in the tax base against which this tax rate would be applied. Similarly, there could be a redefinition of income with no change in the average level of tax rates nor in the progressivity of the tax system. Of course, to change one without changing the other may have implications for the total amount of revenue which the government collects although that also is not necessarily the case.

2. WHY CHANGE THE TAX SYSTEM?

Raise more revenue

There are, of course, many motivations for wanting to change a tax system. The first and most important reason seems to be the desire to raise more revenue from the existing tax base. But, such an objective may not be compatible with changing the system. The 1981 experience in Canada suggests that the political response may vitiate the attempt to combine these objectives. Those who stood to lose tax avoidance privileges available under the current system of taxation were able to mount a very effective lobby to inhibit the changes. Also because the tax changes proposed in the November 1981 budget did collect extra revenue and dismantled whole sections of the existing Tax Act, it would have had a profound economic effect on the system, one which was not desirable at the time.

There are other reasons for wanting to change both the tax structure and the definition of taxable income within the tax system and the reasoning in the United States has tended to focus, not upon the revenue raising aspects but rather, on these other objectives for change.

Incentive effects

Principal amongst these are the effects which the existing tax system has on incentives. It has for a long time been understood that the imposition of a tax changes economic as well as social behaviour. A tax has those effects because it increases the costs of activities which are taxed. For example, at the moment in Canada there are extensive layers of taxation levied on gasoline. The effect is to raise the price of gasoline much above the level which it would otherwise reach and to reduce the demand for gasoline. As the price of gasoline has increased people have chosen to use less of it -- to use their cars less, to travel less, and when they do travel to use alternative modes of transportation.

In the same way, tax reductions on particular items tend to encourage their consumption or use. For example, a reduction in the tax on alternative energy sources such as coal stoves and other implements, has increased the demand for these above the level which otherwise would have been achieved. The fact that capital gains on principal residences are not taxed means that people put more of their wealth into this form than otherwise they would.

The tax system is littered with these sticks and carrots to economic behaviour in the form of differential tax rates.

The effect on work/leisure choices

One of the most important impacts of taxation -- one which has acquired prominence in recent years -- is the effect which taxes have on the choice between income and leisure. The fact that income is taxed means that the relative cost of leisure is reduced. Evidently, if there were no tax on income then the decision to give up an hour of work time for leisure time would be more costly than if the income is taxed at a rate of 50 per cent. An important characteristic of the tax on income and, therefore, the tax which affects peoples' choices between work and leisure is the fact that it is progressive. The more an individual works and therefore the more income an individual earns, the higher the rate of tax to which that income is subjected.

Tax progression reduces effort

While the progressive income tax is justified on a number of grounds, among which is a notion of equity, there can be no denying the fact that such a tax system will cause taxpayers to work less hard than they would otherwise. That is to say, those taxpayers who are influenced in their decision-making by the price of things will choose to work less under a system of progressive taxation.

Let us suppose that under a system of progressive taxation, the rate of tax increases by one per cent for every $1,000 increase in incomes -- a very harsh rate of progression. Under such a system, an individual making $20,000 per year would face a 20 per cent tax rate. If the person's income increased to $25,000 a year the tax rate would increase to 25 per cent. If, on the other hand, a system of flat rate taxation of 20 per cent of income were in effect, the individual would pay the same 20 per cent on the $20,000 per year as they would on the $25,000 per year. Obviously, the individual has less incentive to make $25,000 per year if 25 per cent of it will be taxed than he does if 20 per cent of it will be taxed. But, willingness to earn more income or the desirability of earning more income obviously has implications for the extent of productivity in the economy and ultimately for the amount of tax revenue which government can collect since tax revenue is determined by the size of the tax base as well as by the tax rate which government imposes. Evidently, if people work less the economy is less productive and there is a smaller tax base from which government can extract taxes.

So, one of the reasons for wanting to change an existing system of taxation is because of the effects which that tax system is having on economic behaviour and also on social behaviour.

The search for tax neutrality

The most often cited goal of economists in proposing tax regimes or changes in tax regimes is the desire of achieving tax neutrality. That is to say, of arriving at a tax system which has no effect on the choices which individuals make in the marketplace or has as little effect as possible on those choices. At least some of the opinion of economists centres on the view that there is no such thing as neutral taxation, that any tax will fundamentally change the economic system and that tax neutrality is an ephemeral, unachievable objective. Whether that is true or not, it is obviously the case that, for example, a flat-rate tax system would be more neutral in this sense than a progressive tax system since it would treat people of all incomes equally and, hence, not have a changing effect on economic behaviour as income changed.

Current tax system inhibits the Horatio Alger effect

A flat-rate tax system would also have fewer inhibitory effects on work effort since it would not change the relative price of leisure as income increased such as is the case under a progressive tax system. For example, under a flat-rate tax system, individuals with incomes of $10,000 per year and $100,000 would pay the same proportion of their income in tax. Under a progressive tax system, on the other hand, an individual Horatio Alger would face an enormous tax burden in moving from one level of income to another. For example, the Canadian Horatio Alger starting out at an income of $10,000 in 1971 would have paid a combined federal and provincial tax of $2,177 or an average tax of 21.77 per cent. If, by 1981, the same individual had increased his income to $100,000 he would have faced a total tax bill for income tax of $43,106 -- a tax rate of 43.106 per cent. In other words, under a progressive tax system , the taxpayer would have experienced a doubling of his tax rate and a twenty-fold increase in the total amount of tax payable. Under a flat-rate tax system, the tax rate at $100,000 would be the same as at $10,000 and, hence, the individual would pay taxes of only $21,770 with an income of $100,000. A total difference of $21,336.

Defining the tax base -- what gets taxed?

One of the objectives of the ill-fated MacEachen budget of 1981 was to review the comprehensivity of the tax base and to change the approach to its definition. The tax base, which in principle consists of all earned income, has been whittled down over the years because of a number of government policies giving special tax treatment to income which is expended in particular ways. Thus, taxpayers have been able to earn exemption from taxation or special tax deductions by spending their income in particular ways. Money spent, for example, in drilling for oil or manufacturing Canadian movies or doing high technology research and development acquires special tax treatment in the sense that these expenditures can be deducted from income in determining taxable income. More prosaic activities such as retirement savings have also been accorded special tax treatment.

The effect of all of these so-called loopholes or incentive programs, has been to make the tax system very complex and to make the opportunities for tax avoidance very high for those willing to expend the effort to investigate the possibilities. Of course, the tax saving via these incentive programs is very often more apparent than real since there are many dollars used up in the process of taking advantage of them. Many concerns have also been expressed about the fact that, within particular income groups, individuals with the same income are being assessed very different tax bills because of the possibility of some to shelter their income and, hence, avoid taxation altogether. Thus, within a group of individuals with the same incomes or within a range of $5,000 there might be a wide variance in the actual effective tax paid because of the varying extent to which individuals avail themselves of these tax avoidance possibilities.

Tax incentives distort the economy

As has often been noted by economists, one of the problems with these tax incentive programs is that they channel money into a particular area of investment or spending to an extent that may not be warranted by the underlying economic circumstances. For example, if the rate of return in Canadian film making is really below the market level and, hence, does not encourage natural investment in this area, the existence of a tax incentive may cause Canadians to allocate investment funds into this industry whereas investment is not warranted. The elimination of the tax incentive programs over a period of time would, therefore, cause the actual allocation of capital in Canada to more closely approximate the most effective allocation because capital allocation would be directed by rates of return determined in the marketplace.

Tax system not uniform

Although the tax system appears to be uniformly applied across individuals, the fact of the matter is that it affects Canadians very differently according to their activities and other attributes. As is well known, there are exemptions for age and for children, deductions for interest from savings accounts, special treatment of those who have capital gains or receive income in the form of dividends from Canadian corporations. Simplifying the tax system, therefore, would have the effect of making it more uniform since to the extent that tax incentives or tax deductions were not provided there would be a limited possibility for individuals with the same income to pay dissimilar amounts of tax.

It is important to recognize, however, that the exemptions and deductions which at any point in time are available in the tax system, have an effect on the extent of tax burden which is borne by different income groups. Thus, for example, the fact that individuals can shelter income from taxation by disposing of their income in a certain way, yields a different progressivity of the tax system than is implied by the legislated tax rates. Progressivity in tax rates can be wholly or in part offset by progressivity of deductions. As we shall see in the next section, this is a characteristic of the Canadian tax system.

3. CHARACTERISTICS OF THE CANADIAN TAX SYSTEM

Who files tax returns?

For the purposes of the analysis in this monograph, we have divided the taxpaying public into income groups ranging from $1,000 to $200,000 and over in total assessed income. These 12 groups range in average assessed income from $3,062 for the lowest to $361,287 for the highest group. As is evident from Chart One, however, the

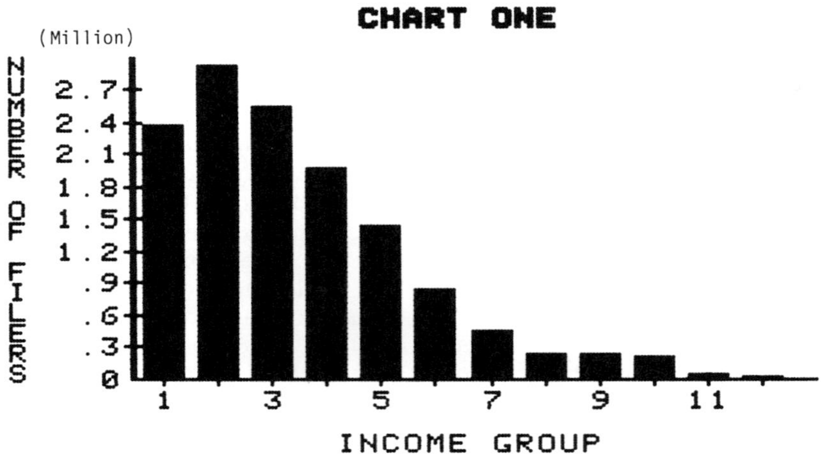

Source: Table I

Income Groups:

1. $ 1-5,000
2. $ 5-10,000
3. $10-15,000
4. $15-20,000
5. $20-25,000
6. $25-30,000
7. $30-35,000
8. $35-40,000
9. $40-50,000
10. $50-100,000
11. $100-200,000
12. $200,000 +

preponderance of the tax-filers fall within the first six income groups. In fact, only a negligible number of Canadians fall within the top six. It is worth mentioning, however, that this income grouping is done on an individual basis in keeping with the requirement that individual income-earners file separate tax returns in Canada. So, no easy relationship can be made between the information on tax-filers and family income groupings which is the more usual way in which we refer to income distribution in Canada. For purposes of this analysis, both because the data are more readily available in that form and because it does seem appropriate to focus on those who actually pay income tax when doing an analysis of tax systems, we have restricted our attention to the tax-filer data.

Who earns the income?

Not surprisingly the distribution of tax-filers is reflected in the distribution of income reported by the various income groups. However, as can be seen from Chart Two the distribution of

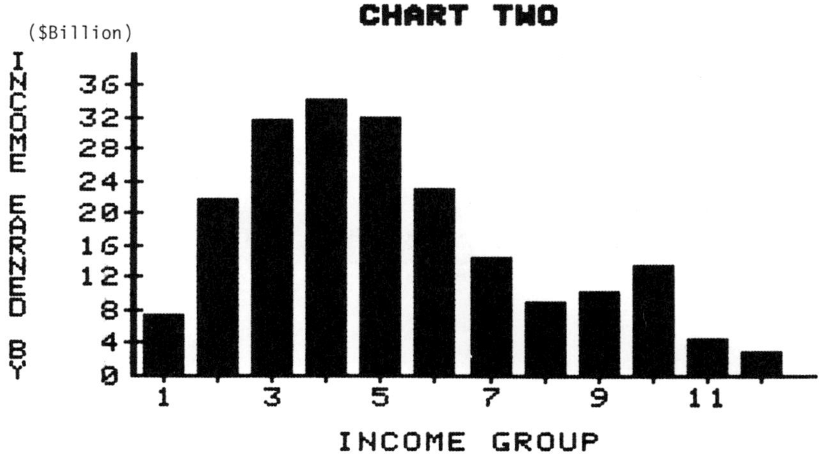

Source: Table I

Income Groups:

1. $ 1-5,000
2. $ 5-10,000
3. $10-15,000
4. $15-20,000
5. $20-25,000
6. $25-30,000
7. $30-35,000
8. $35-40,000
9. $40-50,000
10. $50-100,000
11. $100-200,000
12. $200,000 +

income is somewhat shifted by comparision with the distribution of tax-filers. The distribution is what economists call 'bi-modal' in that there are two distinct groupings of income distribution -- one around the fifth income group and one around the tenth income group. However, it is quite clear that the bulk of income is earned by those in income groups below the eighth with an average income of $37,233 per year or less.

Chart Three presents the distribution of the total tax burden and it is not surprising to find, given that the group below $37,000 earned most of the income in the country, that this group also pays the lion's share of the taxes. In fact, 75.6 per cent of all income taxes are paid by those in groups one to eight whose average overall income was only $13,300.

CHART THREE

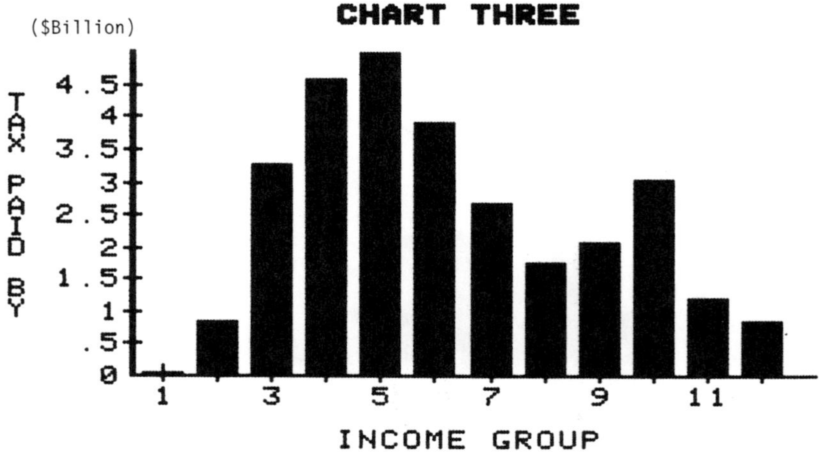

Source: Table I

Income Groups:

1. $ 1-5,000	5. $20-25,000	9. $40-50,000
2. $ 5-10,000	6. $25-30,000	10. $50-100,000
3. $10-15,000	7. $30-35,000	11. $100-200,000
4. $15-20,000	8. $35-40,000	12. $200,000 +

Characteristics of income earners

The impression conveyed by these charts may not lead us to draw the appropriate conclusion and it is, therefore, worthwhile examining at least to some extent, the characteristics of the income groups. The most important thing to recognize about these charts is that they are a snapshot in a life process for most of the filers examined. For example, many low-income earners are the young and the old. This means that they are depicted in these figures in an unusual aspect of their life circumstance. For example, a total of 6,410,537 of the returns filed out of a total of 14,764,878 were filed by Canadians who were less than 30 years of age or more than 65 years of age. In other words, 43 per cent of the income tax returns filed are filed by individuals who either have not yet reached their career average incomes or are beyond the age of retirement. As we shall see in a subsequent section, this has implications for the perceived incidence of the income tax burden and the attractiveness of the flat- rate tax proposal.

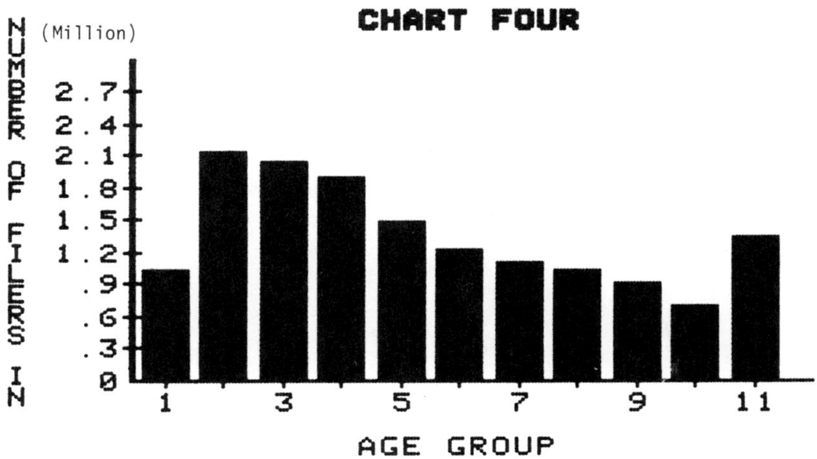

Source: Table I

Age Groups.

0 - 20 years	30 - 35 years	50 - 59 years
20 - 24 years	40 - 44 years	60 - 64 years
25 - 29 years	45 - 49 years	65+
30 - 34 years	50 - 54 years	

It is of particular interest to note that of the 7,839,835 tax-filers whose income was less than $15,000 in 1980, 63.8 per cent of them or 4,965,709 were either less than the age of 30 or beyond the age of retirement. The importance of this distribution of age in the income distribution can be more readily perceived from Chart Five which displays the relationship between average income and age for those tax-filers who actually had to pay income tax. As can be seen, the average profile rises from an income of only $9,121 for those less than age 20 up to a peak average of $22,757 for those age 50-54 and then down again to an average income of $20,249 for those who are age 70 or more. It is again perhaps useful to note that these average income figures include both full

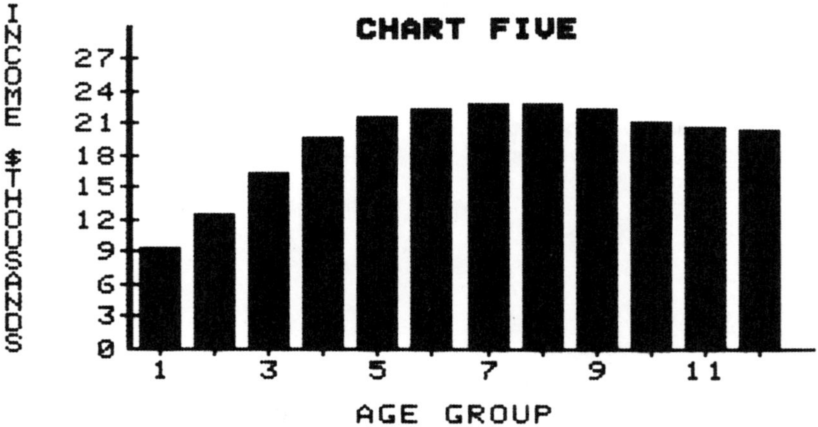

Source: Table I

Age Groups.

0 - 20 years
20 - 24 years
25 - 29 years
30 - 34 years
30 - 35 years
40 - 44 years
45 - 49 years
50 - 54 years
50 - 59 years
60 - 64 years
65+

and part-time workers, and that the average earnings of full-time workers in each of the age categories would be somewhat higher.

Who pays the tax?

As can be seen from Table I and Chart Three, the bulk of the total income tax burden is borne by income earners whose average income ranges from $12,400 to $32,200. Those in this particular income range bear 66.5 per cent of the total tax burden. Just over three per cent is paid by those whose incomes were less than $10,000 while the remainder was paid by those whose incomes exceeded $35,000.

Theoretical versus average actual

This pattern of tax burden distribution is produced by the interaction of rising income with a progressively structured rate schedule. The rate schedule for the year 1980 is displayed in Table II. It can be seen in that table that the theoretical rate of

TABLE I

BASIC DATA FOR TAX ANALYSIS - 1980

Income Groups	1000 TO 5000	5000 TO 10000	10000 TO 15000	15000 TO 20000	20000 TO 25000	25000 TO 30000	30000 TO 35000	35000 TO 40000	40000 TO 50000	50000 TO 100000	100000 TO 200000	200000 +	TOTAL
TOTAL INCOME	7264045	21759262	31539132	33946147	31992177	22725391	14203597	8706290	10094816	13238327	4248255	2797083	2.0251E8 *
PERSONAL EXEMPTIONS	7794004	10453181	9419232	7726340	6078410	3696649	2001320	1081330	1054507	939460	142838	32499	50419770
TOTAL DEDUCTIONS	1160263	2993221	4199453	4505227	4165599	2995598	1917493	1202942	1399388	1927788	695240	738859	27901071
TAXABLE INCOME	639038	8535189	17952325	21728037	21759539	16042677	10290295	6426218	7644942	10378574	3414779	2028464	1.2684E8 *
FEDERAL TAX PAYABLE	925	625918	2326238	3336532	3623276	2811546	1892911	1237551	1550201	2255686	867630	613155	21141569
PROVINCIAL TAX PAYABLE	3315	303678	919363	1250695	1362141	1080349	751852	488269	506118	761208	318629	225015	7970632
NUMBER OF FILERS	2372280	2925664	2542119	1949736	1435101	834288	440951	233833	227638	206311	32597	7742	13208260
AVERAGE INCOME	3062.052	7437.376	12406.63	17410.64	22292.63	27239.26	32211.28	37232.94	44345.92	64166.85	130326.6	361286.9	15.33241
AVERAGE TAXABLE INCOME	269.3771	2917.351	7061.953	11144.09	15162.37	19229.18	23336.60	27482.08	33583.77	50305.48	104757.5	262007.7	9603.088
% INCOME EARNED BY GROUP	3.586925	10.74454	15.57376	16.76233	15.79747	11.22161	7.013619	4.299094	4.984737	6.536977	2.097753	1.381177	100.
% DEDUCTIONS CLAIMED BY GRP	4.158489	10.72798	15.05123	16.14715	14.92939	10.73650	6.872471	4.311455	5.015535	6.909369	2.491804	2.648138	100.
% EXEMPTIONS CLAIMED BY GRP	15.45823	20.73231	18.68162	15.32403	12.05561	7.331745	3.969316	2.144655	2.091455	1.863277	.2832976	.0644569	100.
% FILERS IN GROUP	17.96058	22.15026	19.24643	14.76149	10.86518	6.316411	3.338449	1.770354	1.723452	1.561985	.2467925	.0586148	100.
AVERAGE TOTAL TAX RATE (BASED ON TAXABLE INCOME)	.6634973	10.89133	18.07900	21.11202	22.91141	24.25964	25.70153	26.85592	26.89777	29.06848	34.73897	41.32043	22.95189
EXEMPTIONS % GROSS INCOME	107.2956	48.04014	29.86522	22.76058	18.99963	16.26660	14.09023	12.42010	10.44602	7.096516	3.362275	1.161889	24.89687
DEDUCTIONS % GROSS INCOME	15.97268	13.75608	13.31506	13.27169	13.02068	13.18172	13.50005	13.81693	13.86244	14.56217	16.36531	26.41534	13.77732
% TAX PAID BY INCOME GROUP	.0145643	3.193149	11.14859	15.75706	17.12484	13.36860	9.084724	5.928167	7.063427	10.36299	4.074783	2.879102	100.

Note: * Figures in 100's of Billions.

Source: Taxation Statistics 1982 Edition, Analyzing the Returns of Individuals for the 1980 Taxation Year and Fraser Institute calculations.

Table II

Personal Income Tax: Federal and Provincial Marginal Rates 1980

Taxable income, $	Combined marginal rates, %									
	Nfld.	P.E.I.	N.S.	N.B.	Que.	Ont.	Man.	Sask.	Alta.	B.C.
1	3.48	3.07	3.15	3.15	12.81	–	–	–	–	–
578	3.48	3.07	3.15	3.15	13.79	–	–	–	–	–
904	9.28	8.19	8.40	8.39	13.79	–	–	–	–	–
1,245	9.28	8.19	8.40	8.39	14.78	–	–	–	–	–
1,806	9.86	8.70	8.93	8.92	14.78	–	–	–	–	–
1,813	26.86	25.70	25.93	25.92	28.98	24.48	26.18	–	–	24.48
2,016	26.86	25.70	25.93	25.92	29.96	24.48	26.18	–	–	24.48
2,412	26.86	25.70	25.93	25.92	29.96	24.48	26.18	26.01	–	24.48
2,740	26.86	25.70	25.93	25.92	29.96	24.48	26.18	26.01	–	24.48
2,907	26.86	25.70	25.93	25.92	30.95	24.48	26.18	26.01	–	24.48
3,613	28.44	27.21	27.45	27.44	31.78	25.92	27.72	27.54	–	25.92
3,688	28.44	27.21	27.45	27.44	31.78	25.92	27.72	27.54	24.93	25.92
3,937	28.44	27.21	27.45	27.44	32.76	25.92	27.72	27.54	24.93	25.92
5,128	28.44	27.21	27.45	27.44	33.75	25.92	27.72	27.54	24.93	25.92
5,419	30.02	28.73	28.98	28.97	34.59	27.36	29.26	29.07	26.32	27.36
6,505	30.02	28.73	28.98	28.97	35.57	27.36	29.26	29.07	26.32	27.36
7,930	30.02	28.73	28.98	28.97	35.57	27.36	29.26	29.07	26.32	27.36
8,096	30.02	28.73	28.98	28.97	36.56	27.36	29.26	29.07	26.32	27.36
9,031	33.18	31.75	32.03	32.01	38.23	30.24	32.34	32.13	29.09	30.24
9,248	33.18	31.75	32.03	32.01	38.23	30.24	32.34	32.13	29.09	30.24
9,936	33.18	31.75	32.03	32.01	39.21	30.24	32.34	32.13	29.09	30.24
12,062	33.18	31.75	32.03	32.01	40.20	30.24	32.34	32.13	29.09	30.24
12,389	31.29	29.86	30.14	30.12	38.62	28.35	30.45	30.24	27.20	28.35
12,643	34.27	32.70	33.01	32.99	40.14	31.05	33.35	33.12	29.79	31.05
14,520	34.27	32.70	33.01	32.99	41.12	31.05	33.35	33.12	29.79	31.05
16,255	37.25	35.55	35.88	35.86	42.64	33.75	36.25	36.00	32.38	33.75
17,361	37.25	35.55	35.88	35.86	43.63	33.75	36.25	36.00	32.38	33.75
19,867	41.72	39.81	40.18	40.17	45.91	37.80	40.60	40.32	36.26	37.80
20,645	41.72	39.81	40.18	40.17	46.89	37.80	40.60	40.32	36.26	37.80
24,442	41.72	39.81	40.18	40.17	47.88	37.80	40.60	40.32	36.26	37.80
25,285	47.68	45.50	45.92	45.90	50.92	43.20	46.40	46.08	41.44	43.20
25,377	50.56	48.38	48.80	48.78	53.32	46.08	49.28	48.96	44.32	46.08
28,830	50.56	48.38	48.80	48.78	54.30	46.08	49.28	48.96	44.32	46.08
31,601	50.56	48.38	48.80	48.78	54.30	46.08	49.28	50.66	44.32	46.08
33,902	50.56	48.38	48.80	48.78	55.29	46.08	49.28	50.66	44.32	46.08
39,767	50.56	48.38	48.80	48.78	56.27	46.08	49.28	50.66	44.32	46.08
43,345	56.88	54.43	54.90	54.88	59.61	51.84	55.44	56.99	49.86	51.84
46,545	56.88	54.43	54.90	54.88	60.60	51.84	55.44	56.99	49.86	51.84
54,381	56.88	54.43	54.90	54.88	61.58	51.84	55.44	56.99	49.86	51.84
60,715	56.88	54.43	54.90	54.88	62.57	51.84	55.44	56.99	49.86	51.84
70,435	61.62	58.96	59.48	59.46	65.08	56.16	60.06	61.74	54.02	56.16
108,361	67.94	65.01	65.58	65.55	68.42	61.92	66.22	68.07	59.56	61.92

Source: *The National Finances*, Canadian Tax Foundation, 1980-81, p. 69.

Table III

Assessed Income	Tax Payable	Tax Rate
$	$	%
1,500		
2,000		
2,500		
5,000		
7,500	648	8.64
10,000	1,270	12.70
12,500	1,912	15.30
15,000	2,624	17.49
17,500	3,368	19.25
20,000	4,144	20.72
25,000	5,876	23.50
30,000	7,831	26.10
50,000	17,206	34.41
100,000	44,234	44.23
200,000	105,448	52.72

Source: The National Finances, Canadian Tax Foundation, 1980-81.

taxation, depending on the province of residence, varies from 3.48 per cent on the first dollar of taxable income to 68.42 per cent. These are the rates of tax which apply on each additional dollar earned above the noted taxable income. For a single taxpayer with no dependents, the application of these tax rates would yield the theoretical average tax rates shown in Table III. However, from the actual tax forms filed we discover $200,000 income range varies only from just over half of one per cent to 34.7 per cent. The average actual total tax rate on taxable income amounted to 22.95 per cent. The reason for the difference between the theoretical tax rate and the tax rate actually faced by income earners is due to the existence of exemptions and deductions.

The crucial role of deductions and exemptions

Chart Six displays exemptions and deductions as a fraction of gross income. As can be seen, in the case of low income earners, personal exemptions from taxation amount to very significant

CHART SIX

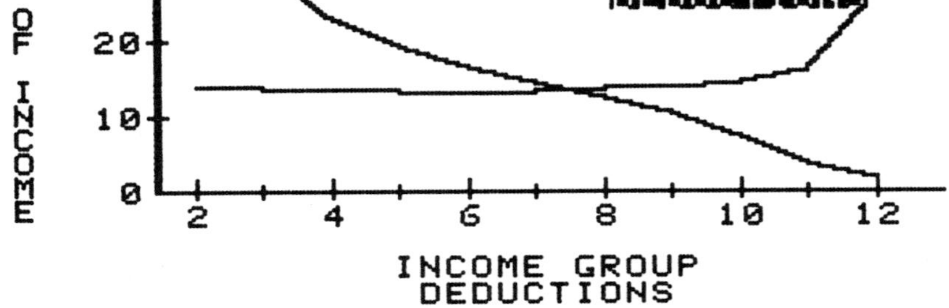

Source: Table I

fractions of total income earned. In the case of deductions, the amount of income sheltered varies from a low of 13.02 per cent at an average income level of $22,292 to a high of 26.42 per cent at an income level averaging $361,287. In other words, the steeply progressive rate structure as provided for in legislation is offset by other tax provisions permitting income sheltering through deductions and the exemption of income by the various exemptions available.

As I pointed out above, the bulk of the tax is paid by the income group whose income ranged from $10,000 to $35,000. It is interesting to note that within this group which paid two-thirds of the total tax bill in 1980 there is a negligible amount of variation in the average tax rate. The tax rate for the lowest group within that income range was 18.1 per cent while the top rate was 25.7 per cent. In other words, two-thirds of the tax is paid by an income group which for all intents and purposes faces a flat- rate tax schedule.

4. THE TAX SYSTEM AND THE INDIVIDUAL TAXPAYER

The foregoing analysis has provided an indication of how taxpayers as a group are affected by the tax system as it existed in 1980. In this section we attempt to bring the analysis to life by providing an indication of how income earners at particular income levels fared in that tax system as a prelude to the following section which considers the implications of adopting a flat-rate tax.

Table IV displays the income exemption, deductions, taxable income, and tax status of income earners who were average within each of the 12 groups analyzed in the preceding section. For example, the average individual in the fourth income group had an income of $17,410, average exemptions of $3,963 and average deductions of $2,311. The combination of exemptions and deductions reduced the gross income of $17,410 to a taxable income of $11,137 which attracted tax at an average rate of 21 per cent producing a total tax bill of $2,353. This amounted to 13.5 per cent of gross income earned and amounted to 17.5 per cent of gross income minus exemptions.

TABLE IV

INCOME AND TAXES FOR INDIVIDUALS

$

AVERAGE INCOME	3062.052	7437.376	12406.63	17410.64	22292.63	27239.26	32211.28	37232.94	44345.92	64166.85	130326.6	361286.9
AVERAGE EXEMPTIONS	3285.449	3572.926	3705.268	3962.762	4235.528	4430.903	4538.645	4624.369	4632.386	4553.611	4381.937	4197.753
AVERAGE DEDUCTIONS	489.0919	1023.091	1651.950	2310.686	2902.652	3590.604	4348.540	5144.449	6147.427	9344.087	21328.34	95435.16
AVERAGE TAXABLE INCOME	0	2841.358	7049.413	11137.19	15154.45	19217.76	23324.10	27464.12	33566.10	50269.15	104616.3	261654.0
AVERAGE TAX PAID	0	317.7385	1276.731	2352.743	3473.914	4664.930	5997.861	7380.566	9033.285	14623.04	36391.66	108262.7
TAX AS % OF GROSS INCOME	0	4.272185	10.29071	13.51325	15.58324	17.12576	18.62037	19.82268	20.37005	22.78909	27.92344	29.96586
TAX AS % OF TAXABLE INCOME	0	11.18263	18.11116	21.12510	22.92339	24.27406	25.71530	26.87348	26.91193	29.08949	34.78585	41.37630
TAX AS % OF GR INC - EXEMPT	0	8.222089	14.67277	17.49527	19.23849	20.45272	21.67434	22.63382	22.74611	24.52985	28.89497	30.31812

Source: Table 1 and Fraser Institute Calculations.

The information in Table IV makes clear the important role of exemptions in maintaining a low rate of tax on low income earners while providing for a fairly steep progressivity of the tax system. Exemption levels for low-income earners on average were not much different than the exemption levels of high-income earners. The difference between the low and high-income earners reflects life cycle effects in that the characteristic low income of young people is also associated with single marital status and reflects the fact that the more dependents a taxpayer has the more likely he or she is to be in income classes above the third.

Table IV also underlines the importance of deductions in reducing the tax liabilities of both high and low-income Canadians but especially those who have incomes above the average. These deductions are the practical manifestation of the "incentives and loopholes" discussed earlier. They are also an important source of complexity in the tax system. The attempts by government to direct a stream of tax free income to a particular sector invariably involves a vast array of enforcement devices to ensure that the trickle does not become a torrent. The latter outcome, of course, is the principal effect of the effort of private tax advisers whose interest it is to amplify the applicability and extent of the deductions.

5. ANALYZING THE FLAT TAX PROPOSALS

This section of the paper reports the analysis of a number of flat-rate tax proposals which have been advanced. The proposals vary according to their definition of taxable income and the structure of tax rates which would apply to taxable income so defined.

Four different tax proposals are examined. The first, which is acquiring significant attention at the moment, is that which is being proposed by Progressive Conservative leadership candidate Peter Pocklington. The second is a variant of the Pocklington proposal involving a different definition of taxable income. The third involves a dual flat-rate tax system, whereas the fourth involves a progressivity of tax up to $32,000 of gross income and a flat-rate tax beyond $32,000. The latter proposal is being advanced by Member of Parliament John Evans, Chairman of the House of Commons Finance Committee. The various proposals are summarized in Exhibit One.

EXHIBIT ONE

The Flat Tax Proposals In Brief

	Taxable Income	Tax Rate
Pocklington	Gross income minus exemptions at $12,000 per family of four, $7,500 for single individuals	20%
Simple Flat Tax	Gross income minus exemptions at $7,805.52	19.14%
Dual Tax	Gross income minus exemptions at $7,805.52	17% up to 24,000 taxable income 24% beyond 24,000 taxable income
Evans Tax	Gross income minus exemptions and deductions as under existing tax system	same as under existing system up to $23,324 flat at 30% after

The Pocklington proposal

The flat-rate tax system as proposed by Mr. Peter Pocklington essentially involves a flat-rate of tax applied to taxable income defined as total income minus exemptions. In the Pocklington proposal the exemption level during 1983 would be $12,000 for a family of four and $7,500 for a single individual. In order to test the Pocklington proposal in the context of the 1980 tax data which we have available, it is necessary to translate it into dollar terms which would be relevant for that year. A comparison of the actual family exemptions which were available for 1980 with the proposed level for 1983 suggests that the 1980 level would have been some 39 per cent higher on average than it actually was. Accordingly, to calculate taxable income under the Pocklington scheme for 1980 it is necessary to increase the exemption level by 39 per cent and subtract this grossed up exemption level from actual gross income for that year. Tax payable is calculated at 20 per cent of taxable income. The results of this calculation for taxpayers at different income levels is presented in Table V.

As can be seen, the effect of levying a flat-rate tax at 20 per cent of total income minus exemptions under the Pocklington scheme will be to slightly increase the average taxes paid for all taxpayers with an average income of about $18,000 and below and reduce the taxes payable for all taxpayers above that level. For example, taxpayers in the second income group with an average income of $7,400 paid an average of $317 tax in 1980. If the Pocklington flat-rate tax scheme had been in effect in 1980 these same taxpayers would have paid $494 in total taxes. Whereas in 1980 taxpayers in the second income group actually paid an average tax rate of 4.3 per cent on their total gross income, under the Pocklington scheme their gross tax rate would have been 6.64 per cent on gross income.

The rather modest changes in total tax payable by low-income groups -- the second income group would have paid an average of $187 more -- would, however, yield significant changes in the distribution of the total tax burden. As pointed out in an earlier section, the vast majority of tax-filers have incomes which

TABLE V

FLAT TAX IMPACT ANALYSIS

INCOME GROUPS	1000 TO 5000	5000 TO 10000	10000 TO 15000	15000 TO 20000	20000 TO 25000	25000 TO 30000	30000 TO 35000	35000 TO 40000	40000 TO 50000	50000 TO 100000	100000 TO 200000	200000 +
POCKLINGTON PROPOSALS												
TOTAL INCOME	7264045	21759262	31539132	33946147	31992177	22725391	14203597	8706290	10094816	13238327	4248255	2797083
POCKLINTON EXEMPTIONS (ACTUAL EXEMPTIONS $1.39)	10833666	14529922	13092732	10739613	8448990.	5138342.	2781835.	1503049.	1465765.	1305849.	198544.8	45173.61
INCOME LESS EXEMPTIONS	0	7229340.	18446400	23206534	23543187	17587049	11421762	7203241.	8629051.	11932478	4049710.	2751909.
FLAT TAX AT 20%	0	1445868.	3689280.	4641307.	4708637.	3517410.	2284352.	1440648.	1725810.	2386496.	809942.0	550381.9
FLAT TAX AT 22%	0	1590455.	4058208.	5105438.	5179501.	3869151.	2512788.	1584713.	1898391.	2625145.	890936.2	605420.1
% OF 20% TAX PAID BY GROUP	0	5.315666	13.56346	17.06355	17.31108	12.93159	8.398314	5.296475	6.344860	8.773838	2.977714	2.023453
% OF 22% TAX PAID BY GROUP	0	5.315666	13.56346	17.06355	17.31108	12.93159	8.398314	5.296475	6.344860	8.773838	2.977714	2.023453
IMPACT ON AVERAGE TAXPAYER IN INCOME GROUP												
AVERAGE INCOME	3062.052	7437.376	12406.63	17410.64	22292.63	27239.26	32211.28	37232.94	44345.92	64166.85	130326.6	361286.9
AVERAGE EXEMPTIONS	4566.774	4966.367	5150.322	5508.239	5887.383	6158.955	6308.716	6427.872	6439.016	6329.519	6090.892	5834.876
TAXABLE INCOME FLAT BASIS	0	2471.008	7256.308	11902.40	16405.25	21080.31	25902.57	30805.07	37906.90	57837.33	124235.7	355452.0
FLAT TAX PAYABLE AT 20%	0	494.2017	1451.262	2380.480	3281.050	4216.062	5180.513	6161.013	7581.380	11567.47	24847.13	71090.40
FLAT TAX PAYABLE AT 22%	0	543.6219	1596.388	2618.528	3609.154	4637.668	5698.564	6777.115	8339.518	12724.21	27331.85	78199.44
20% FLAT TAX AS % OF GROSS	0	6.644840	11.69747	13.67256	14.71809	15.47788	16.08292	16.54721	17.09601	18.02717	19.06529	19.67699
22% FLAT TAX AS % OF GROSS	0	7.309324	12.86721	15.03981	16.18990	17.02567	17.69121	18.20193	18.80561	19.82989	20.97182	21.64469
TAX PAYABLE DIFFERENCE 20%	0	176.4632	174.5311	27.73703	-192.864	-448.868	-817.348	-1219.55	-1451.90	-3055.57	-11544.5	-37172.3
TAX PAYABLE DIFFERENCE 22%	0	225.8834	319.6573	265.7850	135.2408	-27.2619	-299.297	-603.452	-693.767	-1898.83	-9059.81	-30063.3
SIMPLE FLAT TAX PROPOSAL												
FLAT TAX AT 19.14% OF INCOME LESS ACTUAL EXEMPTIONS	0	2163984.	4233749.	5018471.	4959895.	3642101.	2335516.	1459417.	1730315.	2354003.	785776.8	529141.4
% OF 19% TAX PAID BY GROUP	0	7.433577	14.54350	17.23913	17.03791	12.51111	8.022813	5.013296	5.943866	8.086319	2.699250	1.817672
IMPACT ON AVERAGE TAXPAYER IN INCOME GROUP												
FLAT TAX	0	739.6556	1665.441	2573.923	3456.130	4365.520	5296.543	6241.281	7601.170	11409.97	24105.80	68346.86
TAX AS % OF GROSS INCOME	0	9.945116	13.42380	14.78362	15.50346	16.02657	16.44313	16.76279	17.14063	17.78173	18.49646	18.91761
TAX PAYABLE DIFFERENCE	0	421.9172	388.7103	221.1807	-17.7841	-299.410	-701.319	-1139.29	-1432.12	-3213.07	-12285.9	-39915.9

Source: Table I and Fraser Institute calculations.

fall in the first seven income groups. As a consequence, although the effect of the Pocklington flat-rate tax would be quite modest in terms of the dollar amount of tax increase implied for the average taxpayer, the total amount of tax paid by the lower income groups would be very significantly increased. Under the tax system as it actually existed in 1980, the bottom four income groups whose incomes were below $20,000 paid 30 per cent of the total tax bill. Under the Pocklington proposal this same group would pay 36.9 per cent of the total tax bill.

One problem with the interpretation of the impact of the Pocklington proposal is the fact that it involves the collection of less revenue than the actual tax system in effect in 1980. In order to make the proposal more comparable to the actual tax system, the flat-rate tax was adjusted up to 22 per cent in order to ensure that the same amount of revenue would have been collected under the Pocklington system as was collected by the actual tax system. As can be seen in Table V, this modification does not change the distribution of the tax burden by income group since the same percentage of the total tax bill is borne by each income group. It does, however, change the actual amount of tax payable by each taxpayer. For example, under the equal revenue flat-rate tax of 22 per cent, individuals with an average taxable income of $7,400 would have paid about $544 as opposed to $318 under the tax system as it actually existed.

The most obvious effect of raising the flat-rate of tax is to greatly increase the income level at which taxpayers would be indifferent between the flat tax and the existing system. (In the sense that taxpayers would have paid the same tax under a flat-rate system and under the existing tax system.) Whereas at a 20 per cent flat-tax the cross over point was at an income level of about $17,000, under a 22 per cent flat-rate tax the cross over point does not occur until about $27,000. In other words, with the 20 per cent flat-rate tax every taxpayer with a gross income of $17,000 and above would pay less tax whereas with a 22 per cent flat-rate tax there would be no benefit until an income level of $27,000 had been reached. At that point, total tax as a percentage of gross income would be 17.03 per cent, somewhat less than the 17.13 per cent of gross income actually payable in 1980.

The simplest flat tax proposal

While each of the Pocklington-type proposals involves a shifting of the income tax burden toward lower-income groups, it is clear that they do this to a lesser extent than the most simple flat-rate tax proposals would. The simplest flat-rate tax system would involve the application of a flat-rate tax to gross income minus exemptions with no increase in exemption levels. For the 1980 tax system, this would have implied a flat-rate tax at 19.14 per cent of taxable income defined as gross income minus exemptions. Under this system, the taxpayer with an average income of $7,400 would have faced a total tax bill of $739 which is $200 larger than the 22 per cent Pocklington system and more than double the average tax actually paid by taxpayers at that income level in 1980. It is clearly the case that the boosted exemption level under the Pocklington proposal greatly reduces the incidence of taxes at the lower income levels.

The dual rate tax system

The Pocklington proposal as has been noted, reduces the impact of a flat rate tax on lower-income levels by boosting the exemption level. An alternative approach which has been suggested by several proponents of the flat-rate tax system in the United States is to create a dual tax rate with a lower rate of tax applying to low-income groups and a higher rate of tax applying to high income groups. This section considers the analysis of such a dual flat-rate tax system with a 17 per cent tax rate for those with incomes below $30,000 and a 24 per cent tax rate for those with incomes above $30,000. These tax rates would apply to gross income minus exemptions.

As can be seen from Table VI, if the exemption levels are taken as they were in 1980 the tax burden on low-income groups is higher than those exacted by the existing tax system but less so than would be the case under a flat-rate tax at 19.14 per cent. The lowest tax paying income group would pay an average of $657 as opposed to $739 under the flat-rate tax. The cross over tax rate income level under the dual tax rate system for the low income group is less than $17,000. The upper income cross over occurs at about $50,000. In other words, under a dual tax rate system with a 17 per cent rate at less than $30,000 and a 24 per cent rate for incomes greater than $30,000, the income earners between $17,000 and $30,000 would be better off whereas those below $17,000 and

TABLE VI

DUAL TAX IMPACT ANALYSIS

INCOME GROUPS	1000 TO 5000	5000 TO 10000	10000 TO 15000	15000 TO 20000	20000 TO 25000	25000 TO 30000	30000 TO 35000	35000 TO 40000	40000 TO 50000	50000 TO 100000	100000 TO 200000	200000 +
TOTAL INCOME	7264045	21759262	31539132	33946147	31992177	22725391	14203597	8706290	10094816	13238327	4248255	2797083
TOTAL EXEMPTIONS	7794004	10453181	9419232	7726340	6078410	3696649	2001320	1081330	1054507	939460	142838	32499
DUAL TAX PAYABLE												
(17% UP TO $30,000)												
(24% BEYOND)												
IN TOTAL BY GROUP	0	1922034.	3760383	4457367.	4405340.	3234886.	2928546.	1829990.	2169674.	2951728.	985300.1	663500.2
% OF TAX PAID BY GROUP	0	6.557884	12.83024	15.20832	15.03080	11.03727	9.992055	6.243836	7.402821	10.07115	3.361795	2.263830
IMPACT ON AVERAGE TAXPAYER IN GROUP												
DUAL TAX AT 17<30 24>30	0	656.9564	1479.232	2286.139	3069.708	3877.421	6641.433	7826.057	9531.248	14307.18	30226.71	85701.39
TAX PAYABLE DIFFERENCE	0	339.2180	202.5011	-66.6038	-404.206	-787.508	643.5715	445.4906	497.9624	-315.863	-6164.95	-22561.3
DUAL TAX AS % OF GROSS	0	8.833175	11.92291	13.13070	13.77006	14.23468	20.61834	21.01918	21.49295	22.29684	23.19305	23.72115

Source: Table 1 and Fraser Institute calculations.

between $30,000 and $50,000 would be worse off in the sense that they would have to pay more tax. This fact is quite evident from the distribution of tax burden which shows that the income groups named above would pay respectively higher and lower percentages of the tax burden under the dual flat-rate tax system.

The Evans proposal

The Evans proposal is essentially that the tax system be a blend of progressive and flat-rate tax with the progressive system ending at a taxable income of $11,120 per year and the flat-rate of 30 per cent obtaining above that income level. The proposal is that these tax rates be applied to gross income minus exemptions and deductions as currently available. In order to implement the Evans proposal for 1980, it was necessary to drop the flat rate from 30 per cent to 29 per cent and to apply that rate to taxable income of $23,324 and over. This slightly modified version of the Evans proposal involves implicit tax rates on gross income of 9.3 per cent for income group two to 17.1 per cent for income group six which has $30,000 at its upper limit.

As can be seen from Table VII the effect of the Evans proposal is to exactly preserve tax rates up to the $30,000 income level and from that point on to bring about a modest but increasing reduction in income tax payable. The Evans proposal also changes the distribution of the tax burden.

Although the low-income groups pay the same total dollar amount of tax, this amounts to a somewhat larger fraction of the total tax burden because the total amount of tax collected would be lower under the Evans proposal. The cross over point of the tax burden shift is in the income range between $35,000 and $40,000 per year. Whereas in 1980 the seventh income group (those with incomes between $30,000 and $35,000 per year) paid 9.08 per cent of the total income tax bill, under the Evans proposal they would pay 9.15 per cent of the total tax bill -- a slight increase. Those between $35,000 and $40,000 paid 5.92 per cent of the total tax bill in 1980 --they would pay 5.88 per cent -- a slight decrease. Of course, it is true under the Evans proposal as under all of the other proposals that the relatively few earning higher incomes would enjoy a tax reduction.

TABLE VII

EVANS PROPOSAL IMPACT ANALYSIS

INCOME GROUPS	1000 TO 5000	5000 TO 10000	10000 TO 15000	15000 TO 20000	20000 TO 25000	25000 TO 30000	30000 TO 35000	35000 TO 40000	40000 TO 50000	50000 TO 100000	100000 TO 200000	200000 +	TOTAL
TOTAL INCOME	7264045	21759262	31539132	33946147	31992177	22725391	14203597	8706290	10094816	13238327	4248255	2797083	2.0251E8*
TOTAL EXEMPTIONS	7794004	10453181	9419232	7726340	6078410	3696649	2001320	1081330	1054507	939460	142838	32499	50419770
TOTAL DEDUCTIONS	1160263	2993221	4199453	4505227	4165599	2995598	1917493	1202942	1399388	1927788	695240	738859	27901071
TAXABLE INCOME	0	8312860	17920447	21714580	21748168	16033144	10284784	6422018	7640921	10371079	3410177	2025725	1.2588E8*
EVANS TAX PAYABLE	0	929596	3245601	4587227	4985417	3891895	2600214.	1669296.	2041784.	2884300.	987183.5	599198.2	28421712
% EVANS TAX PAID BY GROUP	0	3.270725	11.41944	16.13987	17.54088	13.69339	9.148689	5.873313	7.183889	10.14823	3.473343	2.108241	100

IMPACT ON AVERAGE TAXPAYER IN GROUP

INCOME GROUPS	1000 TO 5000	5000 TO 10000	10000 TO 15000	15000 TO 20000	20000 TO 25000	25000 TO 30000	30000 TO 35000	35000 TO 40000	40000 TO 50000	50000 TO 100000	100000 TO 200000	200000 +
GROSS INCOME	3062.052	7437.376	12406.63	17410.64	22292.63	27239.26	32211.28	37232.94	44345.92	64166.85	130326.6	361286.9
TAXABLE INCOME	0	2841.358	7049.413	11137.19	15154.45	19217.76	23324.10	27464.12	33566.10	50269.15	104616.3	261654.0
EVANS TAX PAYABLE	0	317.7385	1276.731	2352.743	3473.914	4664.930	5896.832	7138.839	8969.434	13980.35	30284.49	77395.79
TAX PAYABLE DIFFERENCE	0	0	0	0	0	0	-101.029	-241.727	-63.8510	-642.692	-6107.17	-30866.9
EVANS TAX AS % OF GROSS	0	4.272185	10.29071	13.51325	15.58324	17.12576	18.30673	19.17345	20.22607	21.78749	23.23739	21.42225

Note: * Figures in 100's of Billions.

Source: Table 1 and Fraser Institute calculations.

The life cycle effect of the flat-rate tax

A consideration of the static characteristics of the tax system as represented in one year's data, leads to the understanding that the characteristic of all flat-rate tax systems is to lower the marginal tax rates for high-income taxpayers, to reduce the total tax payable for high taxpayers, and at the same time to increase both the dollar tax payable and the share of the total tax burden borne by low-income groups. For many observers and for taxpayers so affected, the adoption of a flat-rate tax system will therefore not appear to be equitable or fair in some sense. However, as was pointed out in the introduction, in order to properly assess the impact of a tax system we have to look at more than a single year's incidence and, in particular, we have to look at the stage in the life cycle of the taxpayers involved in the static comparison.

As was seen in an earlier section, in 1980 some 7,839,835 tax filers had income less than $15,000 and under the various flat-rate tax proposals (with the exception of the Evans proposal) all of these tax-filers would pay increased taxes, depending on income level, amounting to less than $100 to just over $300 depending on the flat tax proposal considered. However, 4,965,709 of these tax filers or 63.3 per cent of the total were less than 30 years of age or greater than 70 years of age at the time the 1980 snapshot of the income and tax process was taken. The importance of this is that 63.3 per cent of tax-filers who would have to pay increased taxes in that one year were not at a typical income level for their lifetime. The fact is that the average income of tax-filers varies quite distinctly with their age level. For example, tax-filers less than 20 years of age had the very low average income of only $9,121. The average for tax filers whose age was between 50 and 54, on the other hand, was $22,757, whereas by age 70 the average wage had again dropped back to $20,249.

The central point is, of course, that the higher tax bill which these low income taxpayers would pay is offset to some extent by the reduction in taxes which might eventuate because of a levelling of the tax progressivity in years beyond the first one. As Table VIII makes quite clear, this is exactly what does happen. All of the flat-rate tax systems, other than the 22 per cent Pocklington variation, lead to a lower lifetime tax bill than that implied by the tax system as it existed in 1980. The Evans proposal for the

TABLE VIII

LIFE CYCLE TAX IMPACT

AGE GROUP OF TAXPAYER	<20	20 - 24	25 - 29	30 - 34	35 - 39	40 - 44	45 - 49	50 - 54	55 - 59	60 - 64	65 - 69	>70
AVERAGE INCOME EARNED ($)	9121	12252	16135	19453	21424	22121	22580	22757	22180	20976	20614	20249
TAX PAYABLE STATUS QUO ($)	642.6528	1246.889	2078.442	2821.780	3274.429	3434.498	3543.104	3585.721	3448.047	3171.544	3088.409	3004.585
TAX PAYABLE POCKLGTN 20%	818.4615	1421.480	2143.600	2757.229	3120.815	3249.389	3335.368	3368.825	3260.273	3038.174	2971.396	2904.066
TAX PAYABLE POCKLGTN 22%	900.3076	1563.628	2357.960	3032.952	3432.897	3574.328	3668.905	3705.707	3586.300	3341.991	3268.536	3194.472
TAX PAYABLE DUAL TAX ($)	924.3670	1453.645	2080.439	2613.942	2930.291	3042.160	3116.631	3145.532	3051.630	2858.386	2800.284	2741.701
TAX PAYABLE EVANS TAX ($)	642.6528	1246.889	2078.442	2821.780	3274.429	3434.498	3543.104	3585.721	3448.047	3171.544	3088.409	3004.585

Source: Taxation Statistics 1982 Edition, Analyzing the Returns of individuals for the 1980 taxation year.

average life cycle individual yields exactly the same tax bill as would be yielded by the existing tax system.

For those variants which produce a net benefit, the benefits are quite significant. For example, the dual flat-rate tax system produces a lifetime benefit of $12,905 for an average individual less than 30 years of age in 1980.

6. SUMMARY AND TENTATIVE CONCLUSIONS

As was pointed out in the introduction, this paper is intended to be a preliminary examination of a number of flat-rate tax proposals and the effects which they would have on taxpayers as a group and on individual taxpayers. The analysis provided in the paper suggests several tentative conclusions about the application of a flat-rate tax system in Canada.

Effects on tax payable

The flat-rate tax system by its very nature tilts the existing tax distribution so that high-income taxpayers currently paying tax, would pay less tax and low-income taxpayers would pay marginally higher taxes, at least in the first year of the application of the program. High-income taxpayers who currently avoid paying taxes altogether by the use of special deductions and exemptions would, under a flat-rate tax system, pay higher taxes than they currently pay. Low-income taxpayers are preponderantly the young and, while in the first year of application of a flat-rate tax these taxpayers would face a marginally higher tax bill amounting to just over $100 to more than several hundred dollars depending on the scheme adopted, over their life cycle the average low-income taxpayer would actually pay less tax under the flat-rate system. The reason for this is that as the income of the young grows over their lifetime they would face a lower and less progressive tax schedule than under the existing system.

Effects on government revenue

The flat-rate tax can provide the same, less or more revenue than the existing tax system to both federal and provincial governments depending on the flat rate selected and the extent to which personal exemptions are permitted. The proposal advanced currently by Mr. Peter Pocklington at a 20 per cent flat rate and the exemption level which Mr. Pocklington proposes, would produce less revenue than the existing tax system. In order to exactly replace federal and provincial revenues under the Pocklington proposal, a flat-rate tax slightly in excess of 21 per cent would be required.

The proposal advanced by Member of Parliament John Evans also does not yield as much revenue to federal and provincial governments as the existing tax system. In each of these cases, however, there would undoubtedly be an improvement in the growth of the tax base because of the adoption of a less progressive tax system. This would occur because people would work harder and because there would be less incentive to avoid income assessment via the underground economy. However, since there are no good estimates of the extent to which there would be such an increase in the tax base, it is difficult or impossible to estimate the amount of extra revenue which would be forthcoming from this source.

Cost reductions from flat-rate adoption

There are, however, a number of definable cost savings from the adoption of a flat-rate tax. For example, the government currently spends half a billion dollars or more in collecting income tax and evidently a flat-rate tax would make possible a gradual reduction in the staffing of taxation centres over a period of time since the amount of documentation and, hence, the amount of calculation and monitoring would be considerably reduced. It is also true that a more simplified tax system would reduce the extent to which Canadians would need to have access to tax services, chartered accountants, and lawyers in the preparation of their tax returns.

In the last year for which data are available, 1978, one in three Canadians did not prepare their own tax forms. Just over three million Canadians paid a tax service or lawyer or chartered accountant to do their tax returns for them. If the three million Canadians who paid to have their return filed for them paid an average of $100, a very modest assumption, the saving would amount to $300,000,000. Of course, it is likely that the average cost of preparing a return is much higher than $100 and there would be a corresponding saving of a larger amount.

While it is not known to what extent the tax returns of low-income taxpayers are filed by tax services, accountants, and others, it is clearly the case that the money which they would save (amounting to about $100) would serve to reduce the net effect of the flat-rate tax on their circumstances. For example, in the case of the 20 per cent flat tax as proposed by Mr. Pocklington, the total increase in tax payable by the lowest income group as compared to the tax they pay under the existing system, is $176 per year. To the extent that these individuals did in fact pay $100 to have their tax forms completed, the net tax payable difference under the flat tax where they would save that $100 would be only $76 dollars.

The cost of tax preparation would, of course, be much higher for higher income individuals who are likely to have more complicated tax returns. This fact becomes particularly relevant in examining the dual tax rate system where individuals in the income group $30,000 - $50,000 are anticipated to pay from $500 - $600 more in taxes because of the tilting of the high-income tax rate. While it is unlikely that the average cost of preparing their tax returns would be as much as the total difference in tax payable caused by the dual tax rate, it is clearly the case that a significant fraction of that amount might be offset by the elimination of the necessity to pay for tax advice.

The only flat-rate system which would not involve a saving from the point of view of the cost of preparation is the Evans proposal which essentially leaves the existing exemption and deduction levels intact in the initial period of application. There would, however, be a saving in this regard under the Evans system as the deductions and exemptions were eliminated over a period of time.

Flat tax and revenue increases

Of the various proposals considered in this paper, two return exactly the amount of revenue currently collected by the government or more. The dual tax rate system, for example, provides slightly more revenue to both federal and provincial governments than is provided under the current system while the flat-rate tax at 19.14 per cent provides exactly the same amount of revenue put to both levels of government. Of course, in each of these cases the extent of deductions and exemptions is less than is available under either the Evans proposal or the Pocklington proposal and that, to some extent, explains why they yield more revenue.

Evidently, because the simple flat-rate tax with the existing exemption levels as well as the dual rate tax provide more tax revenue they would also provide more flexibility in dealing separately with the problem of low-income taxpayers.

An examination of the life cycle impact of the various flat-rate proposals makes quite clear the fact that over time the flat-rate tax would yield less revenue to government than the currently existing progressive tax system. The reason, of course, is that the flat-rate tax provides little or no increase in the average tax rate as the economy grows and, therefore, there is no automatic escalation in the real level of government revenue. In other words, to extract more tax revenue from a growing economy than would be provided by that growth itself, the government would have to increase the rate of tax. While this may be an unattractive political proposition, from the point of view of taxpayers it would make the revenue and expenditure process at both levels of government more transparent.

If, as is alleged by a growing number of observers, lower marginal tax rates will increase the rate of growth of the economy then, of course, the amount of revenue forthcoming to the government under the flat-rate tax may well exceed the amount coming from the currently existing progressive tax system. However, as pointed out above, there do not exist any reliable estimates of the extent of economic growth rebound which would occur under a flat-rate tax system to make accurate estimates of the increase in government revenue which would be forthcoming.

Conclusion

Our final conclusion on the basis of this preliminary assessment must be that a flat-rate tax system is certainly feasible, that it would produce a certain amount of perverse redistribution of the tax burden but that the extent of this redistribution is likely to be less than is often imagined. Moreover, many of these perverse effects are offset by life cycle impact considerations and by a reduction in the cost of compliance with the existing tax system. It is unambiguously the case that a flat-rate tax would reduce the disincentive to work and productivity imposed by the existing tax system and, on balance, seems to be a direction for reform which deserves the very careful consideration of Canadian policymakers.

Appendix

Summary of Federal Legislation on Flat-Rate Tax pending before Congress.

S. 2147 (Sen. De Concini)
- Flat tax rate on all income not to exceed 20%.
- Personal allowance of $3000 for a single taxpayer; $5000 for a married couple; $4500 for a single head of household; and $600 per dependent.
- Requires Secretary of Treasury to propose legislation to implement the Act.

S. 2200 (Sen. Helms) & H.R. 5513 (Rep. Crane)
- Flat tax rate of 10% of all income.
- Increases personal exemption to $2000.
- All deductions, credits, and other exclusions repealed.

S. 2376 (Sen. Grassley) & H.R. 5868 (Rep. Hance)
- Proposes four areas where the U.S. Treasury could apply a flat tax rate: gross income tax; base-broadening tax on income; consumption-based tax; and consumption tax.

S. 2557 (Sen. Quayle)
- No tax on those with incomes below $17,500
- 18% tax on those with incomes of $17,500 to $50,000
- 25% tax on those with incomes over $50,000

S. 2817 (Sen Bradley)
- Sets rate of 14% for single taxpayers earning up to $25,000 or married couples earning up to $40,000.
- Additional progressive surtax of from 6% to 14% for incomes above those levels
- Eliminates 25 deductions, credits, and exclusions.
- Personal exemption increased to $1500.

H.R. 3181 (Rep. Panetta)

- Repeals all itemized deductions for individuals except those relating to production of income or alimony or support payments.
- Substitutes income tax credit for the personal exemption.
- Abolishes the tax schedule for heads of households.

H.R. 4821 (Rep. Hansen)

- Sets flatrate of 14% for all individuals, estates, and trusts.
- Redefines "adjusted gross income" to eliminate deductions for long-term capital gains, moving expenses, retirement savings, and repayments of supplemental unemployment compensation benefits.

H.R. 6070 (Rep. Panetta)

- Sets a 19% tax on gross income, less business expenses.
- Eliminates most deductions, credits, and exclusions.
- Establishes credit of $1000 for an individual: $1000 for a spouse; $200 per dependent; and $200 for those who are blind or over 65.

H.R. 6352 (Rep. Paul)

- Sets a 10% flat tax rate for all individuals.
- Sets a $10,000 personal exemption for all taxpayers.
- Repeals all deductions, credits, and other exclusions.

H.R. 6628 (Rep. Dannemeyer)

- States that the tax rate should not exceed 15% for individuals.
- Permits deductions for charitable donations.

Source: "The State Factor" September 1982, published by American Legislative Exchange Council, p. 6.